Are People Basically Good?

Crucial Questions booklets provide a quick introduction to definitive Christian truths. This expanding collection includes titles such as:

Who Is Jesus?

Can I Trust the Bible?

Does Prayer Change Things?

Can I Know God's Will?

How Should I Live in This World?

What Does It Mean to Be Born Again?

Can I Be Sure I'm Saved?

What Is Faith?

What Can I Do with My Guilt?

What Is the Trinity?

TO BROWSE THE REST OF THE SERIES, PLEASE VISIT: LIGONIER.ORG/CQ

CQ

Are People Basically Good?

R.C. SPROUL

 LIGONIER MINISTRIES

Are People Basically Good?
© 2016 by R.C. Sproul

Published by Ligonier Ministries
421 Ligonier Court, Sanford, FL 32771
Ligonier.org

Printed in China
RR Donnelley
0001121
First edition, fourth printing

ISBN 978-1-64289-060-0 (Paperback)
ISBN 978-1-64289-088-4 (ePub)
ISBN 978-1-64289-116-4 (Kindle)

Cover design: Ligonier Creative
Interior typeset: Katherine Lloyd, The DESK

Scripture quotations are from the ESV® Bible (The Holy Bible, English Standard Version®), copyright © 2001 by Crossway, a publishing ministry of Good News Publishers. Used by permission. All rights reserved.

The Library of Congress has cataloged the Reformation Trust edition as follows:
Names: Sproul, R.C. (Robert Charles), 1939-2017 author.
Title: Are People Basically Good? / by R.C. Sproul.
Description: First edition. | Orlando, FL : Reformation Trust Publishing, 2016. | Series: Crucial questions series ; No. 25
Identifiers: LCCN 2016016328 | ISBN 9781567696981
Subjects: LCSH: Theological anthropology--Christianity. | Sin--Christianity.
Classification: LCC BT701.3 .S67 2016 | DDC 233--dc23
LC record available at https://lccn.loc.gov/2016016328

Contents

Chapter One

The Supreme Paradox

When I was in high school, my biology teacher told me that my value as a person was $24.37. He was adding up the value of all the minerals in the body—zinc, copper, potassium, etc. Today, thanks to inflation, that total would be around $160. That's still a paltry sum. But it is one way to take the measure of a man.

Other attempts to define man have tried to understand him as simply one variety of primate. Desmond Morris once had a best-seller titled *The Naked Ape,* in which he said there are some eighty-nine kinds of primates—chimpanzees, orangutans, gorillas, baboons, monkeys—but there's one that is distinguished from the rest. It is distinguished not so much by its intelligence but by the fact that it's naked. Man is distinct by the fact that he has to manufacture artificial clothes to cover his nakedness. Evidently, man is the only one of these eighty-some varieties of primate that has a problem with nakedness—and therefore he has a problem with guilt. Man is the only creature in all of creation that has artificial garments, and the Scriptures tell us that this is not to keep us warm but to cover our shame.

Blaise Pascal, the French philosopher said, "Man is the supreme paradox of all creation." Man is the creature possessing the highest grandeur in all of the created universe; at the same time, he is the creature that endures the most abject misery of all creatures in the universe. Pascal said man's grandeur is located in his unique ability to contemplate his own existence. Man alone can think of the future and speculate upon or imagine a better life than he currently enjoys or could ever bring to pass, and this is the source of his misery.

As humans contemplate their existence, they always come around to this basic question: What is man? This question has far-reaching implications, and the answer one gives has a profound impact on how one lives. One theologian has said that how human beings understand their own existence determines how they think, how they behave, and the type of culture that they produce; thus, the culture that we live in is a product of our understanding of what it means to be human. In this book, we will explore what Scripture says about the nature of man, including such related topics as the image of God and the reality of sin.

In our day, most attempts to understand what it means to be human do not begin with Scripture but rather proceed from a worldly perspective. The most common definition for a human being—or for what it means to be human—is the scientific name *Homo sapiens*, meaning "wise man." This term, in distinguishing man from all other creatures in the animal kingdom, does so in terms of intelligence or wisdom. In almost every era of Western civilization, philosophers and theologians have zeroed in on man's thinking capacity as the unique element of his identity.

In the early centuries of Greek philosophical inquiry, the overarching concern was in the dimension called *metaphysics*, meaning that which is above or beyond the physical world. Thales, Parmenides, Anaximander, Anaxagoras, and others before Socrates, Plato, and Aristotle, were asking big questions, such as, what is the ultimate substance from which everything comes in the universe? What is the essence of things? What stands above and beyond the physical? These philosophers couldn't agree on what the ultimate reality is. Plato said it is the transcendent world of forms or ideas; Aristotle said it is the essence embedded within the physical form. Ultimately, thinkers questioned the fact that different philosophers, each acute in their thinking, came to radically different conclusions about issues of metaphysics.

Thus, the next great emphasis in philosophy was in the discipline called epistemology, which is the theory of knowing. It undergirds all science. It is the study of the question, "How do we know what we know?" The focus is on how we learn, how we can know anything, whether we know principally through the activity of the mind or through observation, and related questions.

The twentieth century marked a dramatic shift in the whole history of theoretical thought. The dominant concern in philosophy in the twentieth century was in the area of anthropology, or the study of man. Now, the key question is, what does it mean to be a human being? People are concerned about self-esteem, identity, and understanding who we are as creatures. The focal points in Western civilization include issues such as abortion, euthanasia, human relationships, peace, gender, sexuality, and labor/management difficulties. How we address issues in these areas will depend ultimately upon how we define man.

Philosophers have wrestled with this question before. Plato was perplexed by the task of giving a precise definition to man. In the science of taxonomy, to distinguish a bird from a fish or a fish from an antelope, for example, one looks at what is different among them and also at what is similar. For instance, birds and planes both fly through the air. Birds have wings, and planes have wings. But there are differences too. Planes don't have feathers, and birds have to flap their wings to fly. So when we classify, we recognize the similarities and the differences. Plato was challenged in trying to pinpoint the distinctive features that would separate or distinguish a human being from all other forms of life. Finally, he figured it out: he called man a "featherless biped." One of his students got a plucked chicken, wrote a sign across its chest saying, "Plato's man," and put it on the wall at the Academy—and Plato had to start all over again.

Karl Marx described man as *Homo faber*: man the fabricator, or maker. Marx sought to understand the uniqueness of man not in his chemistry or anatomy but in his work habits. Man's whole life revolves around work, and much of the history of civilization, especially the history of warfare, has to do with a conflict over economic forces and the yield of human labor. Humanity's greatest alienation is the alienation from the fruit of labor, which is unnatural, Marx said. So Marx's theory of economics was rooted in the fact that he saw man as a toolmaker. When anthropologists and paleontologists look back into history and try to draw the line between other kinds of primates and human beings, the presence of tools among the fossils becomes very important because man—*Homo faber*—is the one who fashioned tools and used them to increase production.

Homo volens is another way in which man has been described, particularly in the latter part of the nineteenth century in a school called "voluntarism." This view claims that what makes man unique is his capacity to make choices. Friedrich Nietzsche took this idea farther, saying that the real man, the authentic man—the *Übermensch*, the superman—was a person who made his choices entirely on his own, not living by the pressure of what Nietzsche called "the herd" morality. Rather, he defined a master morality. He affirmed his own personal existence and determined to live his life on the basis of his own private choices, because that's the essence of being human.

Edmund Husserl spoke of man's intentionality—that is, the ability to choose with a purpose in view—as being his basic uniqueness. Jean-Paul Sartre, in a more pessimistic vein, concluded that "man is a useless passion." But both Husserl and Sartre focused on the dimension of choices. Sigmund Freud explored the sexual dimension of what it means to be human, and he thought that the central drive that defines all social interactions and all other values is based in an erotic dimension of humanity.

Finally, it has been said—not only by theologians, but also by historians and philosophers—that man is *Homo religiosus.* Part of the identity of humanity is our capacity for religion. But Calvin made the observation that man is a *fabricum idolorum*—an idol factory—so committed to religion that, even if he removes himself from the living God, he will replace his concept of God with a god made of his own hands. Luther, in similar fashion, commented that "Man, if he has no God, will make an idol," because he has to have something.

All of these are different ways of defining man. Perhaps the great error is trying to understand human identity by simply pointing to one activity, when all of these dimensions together make up the full complexity of what it means to be human.

In the Christian faith, we understand what it means to be human through the lens of Scripture. This key question—what is man?—is found even in the Bible, issuing from the pen of David: "What is man that you are mindful of him, and the son of man that you care for him?" (Ps. 8:4).

Notice that David's question does not concern man alone, but man's relationship to God. The proper focus of theology is God—His character, His works, His attributes. But John Calvin said that no one can really understand who God is without first having some kind of understanding of who we are as human beings. Yet, paradoxically, there's no way that we can really understand what it means to be human until we first understand the character of God. So the knowledge of God and the knowledge of man work together; they are interdependent. The Scriptures tell us that man is made in the image of God. In some way, we are like God, so the more we understand who God is, the easier it is for us to understand who we are. And the more we understand what it means to be human, the more insight we can gain about the character of God.

Chapter Two

The Image
of God

There was an article once in a women's magazine that claimed to answer the question, "How does a wife keep her husband monogamous?" The psychologist who wrote it said that an insightful woman understands that when she's dealing with her husband, in one sense she's dealing with three people: the man whom she married is part boy, part adolescent, and part mature adult. It said the wise woman will recognize that she has to deal with all three of these personalities, which compete at times.

Herbert Marcuse wrote a book called *The One-Dimensional Man* wherein he said that no human being is simply one dimensional in his makeup. There is a chemical dimension, and body chemistry influences every life. There is a biological aspect to humanity, including the sexual dimension. Work is very important, and everyone has an economic aspect to his being. There is a sociological dimension, a psychological dimension, an ethical dimension, and certainly a theological dimension. Any attempt to reduce the essence of a human being to only one of those will produce a simplistic distortion of what it means to be human, because human beings are complex.

Perhaps you've seen those inventories of temperament that claim to be able to separate human beings into four basic psychological types. These inventories may provide some insight into general trends or types of personalities, but the great beauty of the diversity of humanity is that there are no two people in the world who are exactly alike, and a dimension that drives one person in one way will drive someone else another way.

According to Scripture, a crucial aspect of what it means to be human is found in the account of the creation of mankind. Humans, male and female, are defined as creatures made in the *imago Dei*, or the image of God. The language comes from Genesis 1:26–27: "Then God said, 'Let us make man in our image, after our likeness. And let them have dominion over the fish of the sea and over the birds of the heavens and over the livestock and over all the earth and over every creeping thing that creeps on the earth.' So God created man in his own image, in the image of God he created him; male and female he created them."

The description of man as made in the image of God implies some important points. First, to call man the bearer of the *imago Dei* differentiates man from God. First and foremost, we are creatures, meaning that we—finite, dependent, derived, accountable—are not God. We may bear the image of God, but the image of God is not God, but subordinate to Him. No mere human being is divine.

The second point is that this phrase differentiates between humankind and all the other creatures in the world. It sets man apart from the animals. This is a major motif in the biblical account of creation: man, though subordinate to God, is given dominion over all of the earth, a position of authority over the rest of the world, as we saw above: "Let them have dominion." God goes on to say to His new creations: "Be fruitful and multiply and fill the earth and subdue it, and have dominion over the fish of the sea and over the birds of the heavens and over every living thing that moves on the earth" (v. 28).

There's a certain sense in which the world is a trust given to man, with all kinds of responsibilities imposed upon him; at the same time, the world is also a support system for man. One of the things for which humans will have to stand trial before the heavenly tribunal is their ecological transgressions. Instead of dressing the garden, tilling and keeping it, we have polluted, exploited, and violated the garden. We'll also have to answer for the fact that fish eggs are more protected than human embryos, and that there are people who worship cattle while others are dying of starvation.

Man is answerable to God; he's ruled by God. He is a creature, but he has a position of responsibility, authority, and privilege over the rest of the world. Yet, even though we are distinguished from creation, ultimately, we are linked to the creation, so that when humankind fell, the whole world suffered. That's why Paul tells us in Romans that the whole creation groans (Rom. 8:19–22). It's groaning in agony, waiting for the redemption of the human race, because when we are redeemed, there will be a new heaven and a new earth.

Man, in his origins, is made in the image of God. But the next question that we must ask is, are we now in the image of God? Humanity was created in the image of God; do we still bear that image?

That's a crucial question, for this reason: one of the great conflicts today is between a theological and a secular understanding of man. This is a difference between evaluating man from a descriptive perspective or from a normative one. To say it another way, it's a difference in understanding what it means to be human from a theological perspective or a phenomenological perspective. The phenomenological perspective says that if you want to know what it means to be human, you need to study human beings now in their normal patterns of activity. Examine behavioral patterns, and on the basis of sufficient research of behavioral patterns, you can arrive at a description of statistically normal humanity and then build an ethic upon that description. This is a kind of "statistical morality," where, for instance, it's decided that if two-thirds of people are involved in premarital sexual activity, it's normal, and if it's normal, then it's human and therefore good.

The biblical, theological view of man is that mankind in its creation is normative, but what we observe in man is dreadfully corrupted and under judgment. Thus, a descriptive analysis of normal behavioral patterns only provides a profile of a normal sinner. Which brings us back to the question at hand: Does that normal sinner still bear the image of God, or has the image of God been lost in him?

While there is debate about that among theologians, there's no debate in Scripture. The Bible unambiguously teaches that, after the fall, something radical happened to humanity (which we will look at later in the book), but whatever happened to mankind in the fall, man still bears the image of God. We know that simply because the Bible describes man as bearing the image of God after the fall; in fact, it comes at a critical point.

The whole impetus for the death penalty in Christianity has always come out of a profound commitment to the sanctity of human life, tracing its roots back to Genesis 9: "And for your lifeblood I will require a reckoning: from every beast I will require it and from man. From his fellow man I will require a reckoning for the life of man. Whoever sheds the blood of man, by man shall his blood be shed, for God made man in his own image" (Gen. 9:5–6). This passage comes after the account of the flood, during which God destroyed mankind because of its wickedness. And yet, He affirms that man was made in His image and continues to bear that image.

In this passage, God is making a statement of necessary consequence; He says if you willfully, maliciously take the life of a human being, your own life will be forfeit. Why? "For God made man in his own image." The rationale God gives for capital punishment is that He regards a malicious assault on a human life, on His image-bearer, as an attack on His own dignity. The death penalty in Old Testament Israel was not optional, because the Israelites recognized that God had declared human life so sacred that He will not tolerate the malicious destruction of it.

Do you see that how we understand the image of God and its significance—how we understand the holy foundation of a human life—will determine how someone thinks about abortion, euthanasia, capital punishment, and other related subjects? There must be consistency. One person who supports abortion rights once told me that a discarded fetus is "domestic sewage." If it is domestic sewage, there's nothing to be concerned about; but if it's human and alive, then we're talking about one of the greatest ethical issues in our day, if not in all of history.

The Bible, then, is clear that man continues to bear

God's image. But the account of man's creation in Genesis 1 says man is created in God's "image" and "likeness." Does that mean that there are two ways in which we are like God—corresponding to His "image" and "likeness"—or just one? Classical Roman Catholic theology has understood that these words refer to two different things: the image is the rational equipment, the ability to think and make choices, that distinguishes us from the other animals, and the likeness is the sense that we are like God. According to Augustine, and then in a more complex way according to Thomas Aquinas, this second sense meant that in creation man was given a particular gift of righteousness. God bestowed this original righteousness—*originalis iustitia*, sometimes called the *donum superadditum* or superadded gift—on Adam and Eve, but it was lost in the fall. Their humanity remained intact, but the original righteousness, the likeness of God, was lost.

Classical Protestantism takes a different view. Protestants have traditionally asserted that the words "image" and "likeness" in the Hebrew form a *hendiadys*, which is a figure of speech whereby one thing is defined using two distinct yet similar words. This is not unlike how Paul wrote, in Romans 1, about God's wrath being revealed "against all ungodliness and unrighteousness" (v. 18). "Ungodliness" and "unrighteousness " are two words that describe one thing. Likewise, the author of Genesis is referring to a particular characteristic of man: that he's made in God's image. Bearing God's image means that we resemble Him.

How do we resemble God? Some reduce it to an abstract dimension: we can think, we can choose, we can love; and God can do these as well. But what uniquely stamps us as bearing the image of God has to do with our ability to mirror and to reflect the character of God. The image that God gave to us, the likeness that He has put in us as creatures, is an ability to show what it means to be holy.

Chapter Three

The Duality
of Man

On the night before Jesus' crucifixion, He gathered with His friends in the upper room to celebrate the Passover. During the course of their conversation, Jesus told His disciples that they knew God the Father because they knew Him. Philip turned to Jesus and said, "Lord, show us the Father, and it is enough for us" (John 14:8). If there was ever a time when we can almost sense frustration in the words of Jesus to His friends, it's in His reply: "Have I been with you so long, and you still do not know me,

Philip? Whoever has seen me has seen the Father. How can you say, 'Show us the Father'?" (v. 9).

One of the most important aspects of the Christology of the New Testament is the motif found throughout the Gospels, and developed further by the Apostle Paul, that Jesus is the new Adam—that is, He fulfilled what it means to be the perfect man and the perfect image of God. Jesus revealed His deity, but He also, in His humanity, shows what the human race was supposed to be. Christ is a restoration of humankind, the image of God in its fullest manifestation, so much so that even in His humanity, Jesus was correct to say, "Whoever has seen me has seen the Father." In saying this, He did not deny His humanity, nor was He speaking only of His humanity. But if Jesus' humanity is a perfect humanity, and if He displays the image of God in its fullest sense, then to look at Him is to behold the glory of the Creator. That's what an image does: it reflects, mirrors, and reveals a likeness, a similitude of the original.

Since the fall, we are left with a difficult question: Do we still bear the image of God, and if so, to what degree? We saw in Genesis 9 that even fallen man—in the days of Noah, as corrupt as the human race had become by then—was still seen as bearing the image of God. In answering this question, historic Protestantism has made a distinction between the image of God in the narrow sense and the image of God in a wider sense.

To bear the image of God in the wider sense means that, even after the fall and our corruption by sin, we still retain our humanness. Our minds have been affected by sin, as have our bodies; we age, we grow ill, we die, and our faculties have been weakened. We can become addicted and enslaved to certain passions, though we were originally made with a volitional freedom. We still have our faculties, however: we can still think and make choices; we still have bodies; and we are alive. We're still human.

In spite of the loss of our innocence, we have not lost our humanity—but what has been lost is what theologians call *conformitas*. That is, we have lost obedience, and as disobedient creatures, we have besmirched and fogged the mirror that was made to reflect the holiness of God, so that now when the animals and the rest of creation look at us, they see people whose behavior does not conform to the character of God. This, the reflection of the character of God, is the image of God in the narrow sense, and this is what has been lost. Later, we will consider what this loss of conformity means—how seriously we have been affected by the fall and how deep the sinful corruption of our humanity penetrates.

First, we must expand on the dual nature of Christ as both God and man. The Mormons believe that God has a physical body, because of their association of man's image bearing with our physical bodies. Over and against this idea, historic Christianity has insisted that God does not have a body, that He is a spirit. Thus, we must locate those aspects that distinguish us as being in the image of God in His spiritual qualities.

However, as important as those nonphysical dimensions are to understanding what it means to be in the image of God, it would be Platonic rather than biblical to assume that our bodies have nothing whatsoever to do with our being made in the image of God. When God made us human, He didn't just create disembodied souls; He didn't set loose minds, wills, or feelings. He made creatures and fashioned them with bodies. If we look carefully at the biblical description of humanity from Genesis to Revelation, we see that the whole drama of redemption is concerned not simply with the soul but with the body also.

In the Apostles' Creed, there's a clause that reads, "I believe in the resurrection of the body." This does not refer only to the resurrection of the body of Jesus, though the creed does affirm that elsewhere. This phrase refers instead to the church's belief that our bodies will be raised. In other words, at the heart of Judeo-Christian theology is a notion that when God created man, He made him soul and body—and when He redeems man, He redeems him soul and body.

Throughout the history of Christianity, alien strands of thought have invaded the church and tried to communicate the idea that there's something evil about the physical, that it's somehow beneath the dignity of God or foreign to the Christian religion to be concerned about man's material welfare. But the Jesus who walked along the shores of Galilee and was clothed in a human body was very much concerned about people—that the hungry be fed, that those without shelter be covered, and that the thirsty be given something to drink. He was concerned about people's eternal souls, and He was also concerned about their bodies. We must account for the physical, for from beginning to end, to be a creature made in the image of God includes having a body. For us to conform to the will of

God and to display His character and holiness requires that our bodies be involved.

There are people who emphasize the intellectual or spiritual, thinking that if they pray or maintain a contemplative posture for six hours a day, then what they do with their bodies doesn't matter, because all God cares about is the soul. But even a cursory reading of the New Testament reveals that much of the law of God concerns how we use our bodies. Thus, even though God does not have a body, we reflect His image by doing works of obedience with our bodies as well as with our souls. In that sense, the body is an integral part of what it means to be made in the image of God.

Often, the physical aspect suffers a severe devaluation among religious people. One of the most ancient of heresies, which predated Christianity, came in the form of Manichaeism and through various forms of Eastern thought. Plato, for example, developed a philosophy called the theory of ideas. He believed that the highest order of reality is not physical but ideal—that is, it is found in the realm of ideas or forms. These forms are the universal, abstract objects that underlie the kinds of objects and concepts that we interact with on a daily basis.

Imagine two different chairs. One is simple, with a metal frame and a seat and back made of plastic. The other is wooden, padded, and ornate. There are obviously differences between these chairs, but there are similarities, as well—both have four legs, for example. Each is identifiable as a chair; despite their differences, we use the same word for both. Plato said that's because everyone has an idea of "chairness" in their minds. It may be that the beautiful wooden one comes closer to that ideal, but Plato said that in the physical manifestation—what he called the receptacle—of the idea, insofar as any imitation is less than perfect, there's always something lacking.

For Plato and the Greeks, anything physical was seen as being less valuable, less perfect—indeed, intrinsically marred. This view had a profound influence in the early Christian church. Amalgamations of Eastern philosophy, Platonism, and Gnosticism married with Christianity, introducing into the church the idea that the body, as part of the physical realm, is bad.

The monastic movement has sometimes seen radical asceticism as a great virtue. In the Middle Ages, some would wear hair shirts or other coarse garments to inflict constant pain upon themselves or undergo disciplines such as self-flagellation. They would deny themselves any of life's basic necessities to show how righteous they were. One danger in this is that it becomes a works-oriented salvation—we save ourselves by mortifying the physical body. In Greek antiphysical philosophy, redemption ultimately is redemption *from* the body. Plato called the body the prison house of the soul, and the highest hope for man would be the disintegration and destruction of the body, so that the soul could be released to live in pure contemplation, unencumbered by any physical influences. Christianity teaches redemption *of* the body, that in the new heavens and the new earth we will have glorified bodies and still be creatures who are body and soul.

Platonism is a form of dualism, meaning there are two equal and opposite forces—in this case, the spiritual and the physical—that are in constant conflict and that cannot be reconciled. Christianity does not teach this with respect to man. When we say that man is body and soul, we do not mean these are in competition or tension; rather, Christianity teaches a *duality*—that is, man is a harmonic unity composed of two aspects, the physical and the nonphysical. There is duality, but not dualism.

A very old error has made a comeback in recent generations, even among evangelical Christians, called the *tri-chotomy* view. It teaches that our humanity is composed of three distinct aspects: body, soul, and spirit. One of the vehicles through which this view has reemerged is Watchman Nee, a Chinese church leader who integrated Eastern thinking into Christian thought. Trichotomy was condemned in the fourth century. Its fundamental basis is that, because the body and the soul are in irreconcilable conflict, the only way they can be brought together is through a third party—a mediator, the spirit.

Biblical justification for this view was claimed to be in Paul's letters to the Thessalonians, where he wrote, "Now may the God of peace himself sanctify you completely, and may your whole spirit and soul and body be kept blameless at the coming of our Lord Jesus Christ" (1 Thess. 5:23). At other times, however, Paul talks about the heart, the mind, the spirit, and the bowels. These are simply terms for different aspects of the immaterial essence. In misinterpreting such passages, trichotomy leads to a distortion of redemption, suggesting that God has to redeem a person one step at a time: first the soul, then the spirit, then the body.

Theologically, we recognize that the Holy Spirit can distinguish between spirits, souls, minds, and consciences, but to simplify it, the church has said that there is a physical dimension to our lives and a nonphysical one. The term for the nonphysical in the Bible is the soul, which includes the mind, the will, the heart, and other aspects.

Chapter Four

The Reality of Our Sin

One word that crystallizes the essence of the Christian faith is the word *grace*. One of the great mottos of the Protestant Reformation was the Latin phrase *sola gratia*— by grace alone. This phrase wasn't invented by the sixteenth-century Reformers. Its roots are in the theology of Augustine of Hippo, who used it to call attention to the central concept of Christianity, that our redemption is by grace alone, that the only way a human being can ever find himself reconciled to God is by grace. That concept is so central to the teaching of Scripture that to even mention it seems like an insult to people's intelligence; yet, if there is a dimension of Christian theology that has become obscured in the last few generations, it is grace.

Two things that every human being absolutely must come to understand are the holiness of God and the sinfulness of man. These topics are difficult for people to face. And they go together: if we understand who God is, and catch a glimpse of His majesty, purity, and holiness, then we are instantly aware of the extent of our own corruption. When that happens, we fly to grace—because we recognize that there's no way that we could ever stand before God apart from grace.

The prophet Habakkuk was upset during one period in Jewish history because he saw the enemies of the people of God triumphing, the wicked prospering, and the righteous suffering. He raised a lament, saying: "Are you not from everlasting, O Lord my God, my Holy One? We shall not die. O Lord, you have ordained them as a judgment, and you, O Rock, have established them for reproof" (Hab. 1:12). He went on to affirm the holiness of God, and how God cannot tolerate evil: "You who are of purer eyes than to see evil and cannot look at wrong . . ." (Hab. 1:13a).

This is anything but characteristic of the human

condition. We *can* tolerate what is wrong. In fact, if we don't tolerate what is wrong, we can't tolerate each other or even ourselves. In order to live with myself as a sinner, I have to learn to tolerate something that is evil. If my eyes were too holy to behold iniquity, I'd have to shut my eyes anytime I was with someone else—and they would see in me a man who has besmirched the image of God.

Habakkuk then asked, "Why do you idly look at traitors and remain silent when the wicked swallows up the man more righteous than he?" (v. 13b). He couldn't fathom how God could endure and be patient with human evil. Yet, we can't tolerate the idea of God's being upset about human evil; we become antagonistic toward the idea of a God who is so holy that He might turn His back from looking at someone or something that is sinful. That is the dilemma that Scripture sets before us: we have a holy God whose image we bear and whose image it is our fundamental responsibility as human beings to mirror—yet we are not holy.

I once discussed the holiness of God with a group of pastors at a theology conference. One of the pastors said he appreciated my teaching about the holiness of God, but he disagreed with what I taught about the sovereignty of God. I said that, though as Christians we should strive to live together in peace and not be argumentative or divisive, the two of us couldn't possibly both be right when it comes to how God's sovereignty works. And furthermore, whoever is wrong is sinning against God at that point of error.

When we sin, we want to describe our sinful activity in terms of a mistake, as if that softens or mitigates the guilt involved. We don't think it's wrong for a child to add two and two and come up with five. We know the answer's wrong, but we don't spank the child and say, "You're bad, because you made five out of two and two instead of four." We think of mistakes as being part of the human condition. But as I said to that pastor, if one of us is wrong, it would be because he came to the Scriptures while wanting it to agree with him, rather than wanting to agree with the Scriptures. We tend to come biased, and we distort the very Word of God to escape the judgment that comes from it.

But to err is human—which is to say, "It's OK." We are so accustomed to our fallenness and corruption that, while our moral sensibilities may be offended when we see someone involved in gross and heinous criminal activity such as mass murder, normal, everyday disobedience to God doesn't bother us. We don't think it's that important, because "to err is human, and to forgive is divine."

This aphorism suggests that it's natural, and therefore acceptable, for human beings to sin. It's implied also that it is God's nature to forgive. If He doesn't forgive, then there's something wrong with His very deity, because it is the nature of God to forgive. But this is as false as the first assumption; it is not necessary to the essence of deity to forgive. Forgiveness is grace, which is undeserved or unmerited favor. We are so accustomed to sin that we do it all the time. We can't define a human being without defining our humanness as fallen, and we can't possibly maintain life itself apart from grace.

How is sin to be understood? Is it accidental or essential to our humanity? The term *accidental* refers to those properties of an object that are not part of its essence; they may exist or not exist without changing what that object truly is. For instance, a moustache is an accidental property. If a man shaves off his moustache, he does not cease to be a man.

On the other hand, *essential* properties are those that are part of the essence of a thing. Remove that property, and it ceases to be that thing. Sin is not essential to humanity, unless someone believes that God made humanity sinful at the beginning. If sin is essential to humanity, then that would mean Jesus was either sinful or not human. So, sin is not essential. Adam had no sin when he was created, yet he was still human. Jesus has no sin, but He is still human. Believers will have no sin when they get to heaven, and they will still be human.

Sin is not essential, but neither is it merely tangential or on the surface of our humanity. Rather, the portrait that we get in the Scriptures of man in his fallen condition is that he is utterly and thoroughly infected by sin in his whole person. In other words, sin is not an external blemish, but something that goes to the very core of our being.

You may have heard the term *total depravity*. It's one of the most misunderstood terms in theology. I prefer the term *radical corruption*. It's not that every human being is as bad as he could possibly be. But radical corruption means that the sinful nature goes to the *radix*, the root or the core of human experience. Jesus said, "No good tree bears bad fruit, nor again does a bad tree bear good fruit" (Luke 6:43). Mankind's tendency is to minimize this sinful condition as much as possible.

One of the theories of sin that I was taught in seminary is that sin can be defined as finitude. To be finite means that we are creatures; there is a limit to our powers and our being. God is infinite, which means that He is eternal in time, boundless in space, and all-powerful. But finitude goes with anything created, because anything that is created is weaker than what created it. The Creator exists by His own power, but humans can't exist by their own power; they're dependent, derived, contingent, and fragile. In this theory of sin, which is found in nineteenth-century liberal philosophy and twentieth-century existential theology, evil is regarded as being a necessary component of finitude: we sin because we are finite.

The philosopher Gottfried Wilhelm Leibniz produced a very intriguing theodicy, which is a rational attempt to justify or exonerate God in light of the presence of evil in the world. He said that there are three kinds of evil in the world: moral evil, physical evil, and metaphysical evil. Moral evil is what we call sin. Physical evil includes disease or calamities caused by natural events—what we call "acts of God." Metaphysical evil, Leibniz said, meant that to be finite is to be metaphysically imperfect, because only that which is infinite can be metaphysically perfect. Anything that is created is, by nature, finite. He also maintained that moral evil flows out of physical evil and/or metaphysical evil—so what's wrong with the world is simply that the world is finite.

Leibniz said that the only way God can make people is to make them finite. The only kind of a world God could ever create is a finite world, because even God couldn't possibly create something infinite. Anything created would be, by definition, finite, dependent, and derived. Thus, Leibniz concluded, the only way God could create mankind and the world is to create them finite. God has done the best He could possibly do; this is then the best of all possible worlds.

The biggest problem with finitude as an explanation for man's fallenness and sinfulness is that it places the blame for man's sin ultimately on God and absolves humanity from any kind of responsibility. It's the ultimate moral cop-out, whereby I say not that the devil made me do it, but worse than that: the Creator made me do it, because He made me finite. To err is human, and since I'm just being human, God is obligated to forgive me.

We are fallen, we are finite, and we do everything that we can to destroy any authenticity there may be to our existence. Some people have psychological disturbances and chemical imbalances that may serve as mitigating circumstances in their behavior—but the heart of the matter is that we, though made in the image of God, transgress His law. God will never judge us for being finite, but He will justly judge us for being disobedient.

Chapter Five

The Depth of Our Sin

A friend once related to me a conversation she had with her six-year-old son. She had asked him, "Do you think that after you grow up, live your life, and die, that you're going to go to heaven?" The boy seemed pretty confident that he would go to heaven, so she probed a bit: "Suppose you were to stand before God, and He looked you straight in the eye and asked, 'Why should I let you into my heaven?' What would you say to God?" The boy thought for a moment, then said, "If God asked me that,

I would say, 'Because I really tried hard to be good.'" Then a puzzled look came over his face and he said, "Well, not *that* good."

That was perceptive for a six-year-old. Most of us harbor the belief that all it will take to be acceptable to God on the day of judgment is to have tried, done our best, and been basically good. But even a six-year-old child, with a limited understanding of the perfection of God and an immature understanding of his own fallenness, had to think twice—and he realized that his goodness was not quite good enough. It's not even a matter of being not quite good enough, because we are not even close to being good enough. Yet, the greatest and most frequent error that human beings make is to assume that they are going to be approved by a holy God on the basis of their own performance.

How do you hope to stand before God? This calls attention to the problem of our fallenness. Anyone would admit that no one's perfect. Very few people will say, "I'm not a sinner"—but to find one person in ten thousand who has a clear understanding of what that means is exceedingly rare.

The Bible teaches that the problem of human fallenness is not merely something on the surface of our lives; it goes deeper than that. How this condition is understood has to do with the matter of "original sin." Nearly every church has some doctrine of original sin, though how that doctrine is understood varies greatly from one group to the next and from one theologian to the next. But at least this much is agreed upon: if we're going to be serious students of Scripture, we have to develop some concept of original sin.

Today, we are taught that man is basically good, that we have imperfections and blemishes, but underneath all the surface problems, everyone is righteous. But the Bible simply does not teach that man is basically good. In his letter to the Romans, Paul writes: "As it is written, 'None is righteous, no, not one'" (Rom. 3:10). This idea runs contrary to everything that our culture teaches. Maybe all he meant is that no one is perfect, some might say. But then Paul goes on to say, "No one understands" (v. 11a). The structure of Paul's writing is in an elliptical, logical progression to a comprehensive description of the human condition. "None is righteous" and "no one understands." Part of the reason why no one ever achieves the standard of righteousness that God requires is because no one understands what the standard is. We're blinded as to what is right and what is wrong.

Paul wrote that the reason we don't know what is right is that we don't understand who God is. "No one seeks for God," Paul says (v. 11b). No natural person, outside of regeneration, searches for God. People are desperately seeking peace of mind, relief from guilt, meaning, significance, and value to their lives. All the while, they're running as fast as they can from God. God is not hiding; it's not that He can't be found. It's not our nature to seek God—it is our fallen nature to flee from Him.

Paul continues: "All have turned aside; together they have become worthless; no one does good, not even one" (v. 12). We tend to see the word *good* as relative, meaning something is judged to be good or bad according to a standard. But sometimes we don't agree on the standard, leading to different assessments. But, according to God's perfect standard of goodness, no one does good.

A man once came to Jesus and asked, "Good teacher, what must I do to inherit eternal life?" (Mark 10:17). Jesus understood that the man had no idea to whom he was talking, so He replied, "Why do you call me good? No one is good except God alone. You know the commandments: 'Do not murder, Do not commit adultery, Do not steal, Do not bear false witness, Do not defraud, Honor your father and mother'" (vv. 18–19). The man replied, "Teacher, all these I have kept from my youth" (v. 20). I've been told practically the same thing repeatedly. But if you live by the Ten Commandments, you will perish by the Ten Commandments, for "all who have sinned under the law will be judged by the law" (Rom. 2:12). I'm not saying you should ignore the Ten Commandments. But Paul wrote that "by works of the law no human being will be justified in his sight" (3:20).

It was this notion, that he could justify himself by his works, that the young man held when he said, "All these I have kept from my youth." His response betrayed a profound ignorance. Jesus could have said, "You don't understand what the law of God requires. You either have a very simplistic view of what is demanded in the law or a superinflated view of your own performance." Instead, He said, "You lack one thing: go, sell all that you have and give to the poor, and you will have treasure in heaven; and come, follow me" (Mark 10:21). The Scriptures say that the man walked away sorrowful, because he had great possessions. Remember, this man had just said that he'd kept all the law of God. In effect, Jesus was saying, "You've kept the Ten Commandments? Well, let's start with number one: 'You shall have no other gods before me.' Now, go sell all that you have." The young man couldn't keep that one; he never even got to "you shall not murder" or "you shall not steal."

Obviously, the rich man was not present for the Sermon on the Mount, when Jesus explained that when the law says, "You shall not murder," it also contains a prohibition against being angry with your brother without cause (Matt. 5:21–22). God will judge you if you hate others, gossip about them, slander them, or even if you're unkind to them. All of that is bound up in the law against murder. And the prohibition against adultery includes everything that is bound up in the complex of adultery (vv. 27–28). Jesus said the great commandment is, "You shall love the Lord your God with all your heart and with all your soul and with all your mind" (Matt. 22:37). There's no one in the world who has kept the great commandment for five minutes; no one's entire heart has been given to God.

Someone may say, "I sacrifice. I give my money to the poor. I do all the right things." But for a deed to be good in the sight of God, not only must it conform externally to the law of God, but it also must flow out of a heart that loves God completely. If any deed I do has the slightest admixture of selfishness, pride, arrogance, or anything else that mars that work, it's not good in the sight of God. Because sin touches everything, Paul was not exaggerating when he said, "None is righteous, no, not one." There are people who think they have enough goodness to satisfy the demands of God—but they have no goodness that meets the requirements God has set forth.

The Apostle wrote: "Their throat is an open grave; they use their tongues to deceive. The venom of asps is under their lips. Their mouth is full of curses and bitterness. Their feet are swift to shed blood; in their paths are ruin and misery, and the way of peace they have not known. There is no fear of God before their eyes" (Rom. 3:13–18). Do you fear God? Do you have a sense of honor and reverence for Him?

God made you, and He made you in His image. In doing so, He gave you a capacity and a need for the reverence of your Creator. You know that God is worthy of your honor, reverence, and adoration—and that it is your moral responsibility to give Him those things. But we've all been so disobedient for so long that after a while we're not even afraid of God. Paul went on to say that it's not simply that we've missed the mark or that we're alienated from God, but that we are actually enemies of God in our natural state (Rom. 5:10).

When we talk about original sin, we don't mean the sin that Adam and Eve committed, but the result of that first sin. Original sin refers to our sinful condition. In other words, we sin because we are sinners; it is not that we are sinners because we sin. Since the fall of mankind, it is the nature of human beings to be inclined and drawn toward sinfulness. David wrote, "Behold, I was brought forth in iniquity, and in sin did my mother conceive me" (Ps. 51:5). Not only do we have life in the womb, we have corrupt life in the womb. At the very moment we're conceived, we have already participated in the fallenness of the human condition. Thus, we are born with a disposition and an inclination to sin. That's what original sin means.

Chapter Six

The Extent of Our Sin

In his autobiography, *Confessions*, Saint Augustine famously prayed, "O Lord, You have made us for Yourself, and our hearts are restless until they find their rest in You." There's another prayer from Augustine that provoked one of the most serious controversies in the history of theology: "Lord, command what You will and grant what You command." Why would Augustine ask God to give us what He commands from us? He was wrestling with the severity of our fallen condition. God commands perfection, and yet we are born in a state of corruption in which it is morally impossible for us, on our own strength and ability, to do what God commands. The only way we can possibly be obedient to the commandments of God is if He helps us in the process by extending grace to us and enabling us to do what He calls us to do.

There was a monk named Pelagius who became very agitated over this prayer, and his response escalated into a major theological controversy. He said, first of all, that God never commands the impossible. If God commands perfection, then that must mean that we have the ability to achieve it and to live with perfect righteousness. Whatever else the fall did to humanity, it did not take away man's ability to achieve perfection, Pelagius said.

God commands belief in Christ. God doesn't invite people to come to Christ—He commands it. It is the moral duty of a human being to submit to the lordship of Christ and to embrace Christ in faith. In the upper room, when Jesus promised to send the Holy Spirit, He said the Spirit would convict the world of righteousness and sin, for having believed or not believed in the One whom God had sent. Yet, Jesus also said, "No one can come to me unless the Father who sent me draws him" (John 6:44). Pelagius considered these passages and said that if God commands people to come to Christ, then every human being must have the ability to respond to the gospel, or God wouldn't put that obligation in front of His creatures. The controversy came down to this question: How much has the fall of man influenced or affected human choices? In other words, does man still have free will?

You won't find the phrase *free will* in the Bible. Some people argue that though the words may not be there, we can certainly find the concept. And we do—in the sense that the Bible says much concerning the responsibility that we have to make choices. But the emphasis in Scripture, in light of original sin, is on human bondage—of man enslaved to his own wicked desires. It's not that man is a servant to the tyranny of God; man is in bondage to himself and his own sinful predispositions. Augustine would say, yes, you have a free will—but that will, and the choices that you make with it, are deeply influenced by who and what you are. We are creatures who are profoundly fallen, and whom the Bible describes as being in bondage to our own sinful inclinations. Augustine made a distinction in this controversy, saying that man has free will, or *liberum arbitrium*, but since he is fallen, he does not have *libertas*, or liberty—moral freedom from addiction to sin. He said that those who are fallen are addicted to sin.

The Bible says that the desires of man's heart are wicked continuously (Gen. 6:5). Augustine was explaining the biblical concept that freedom means the ability to choose what you want, whereas having free will means having the power to make choices according to what you want rather than according to what is imposed upon you by someone or something else. This introduces a new concept called *determinism*, which says that all of my choices are predetermined by something outside of me so that I don't have any real choice in the matter. In opposition to determinism is the concept of *self-determination*. Self-determination still means that one's choices are determined by something, that is, my own desires. Freedom does not mean acting without a reason, or having an effect without a cause; every time I choose something, there's a reason for that choice. No choice is undetermined. Thus, to be free means having the ability to choose what you want, or having your choices determined by your desires.

Not only *may* a free person choose according to his desires, but to be free means he *must* choose according to the deepest desire he has at the moment. We always choose according to the strongest inclination or the greatest desire that we have. We cannot choose against our strongest desires. If someone had a terrible temptation to do something he desperately wanted to do but which was against God's law, but at the last minute he had the moral courage to say no, it would be because in the end his desire to obey God was greater than the draw of the temptation. We always act according to the strongest inclination that we have at a given moment; that's the essence of making choices. That's what freedom is: the ability to choose according to what you want.

This is why Augustine could say man has a free will but he doesn't have liberty. How can both be true? He said man in his fallenness still has the ability to choose what he wants, but in his heart there is no desire for God or the things of God. If he is left to himself, the desires of man's heart are only wicked continuously. His heart and soul are dead to the things of God. That's our natural state; the Bible says that we are dead to the things of God in our fallen condition, because our sinful condition deadens the soul to them. I still have freedom to choose what I desire—but if I don't have any desire for Christ, will I ever choose Him?

So then, why does one person believe and another person

doesn't? Pelagius would say it's because man has options: to embrace Christ or not to embrace Him; to obey God or not. It is within the power of a human being to obey God at every turn without any assistance from God's grace. But Augustine would say man is dead in his sins. He has no desire for Christ, and the only way he will ever choose Christ is if God softens his stone-cold, recalcitrant heart and puts in him a desire for Christ.

Pelagius claimed that Adam's sin injured only Adam; there was nothing passed on to Adam's posterity. Adam's sin was merely a bad example. Augustine, on the other hand, maintained that Adam's sin affected not only Adam but the whole human race. Pelagius said that some are saved by the law, apart from the gospel—they live lives that are good enough to go to heaven. Augustine answered, "By works of the law no human being will be justified." No one can possibly be saved through human merit or works.

Nearly every church tradition has some doctrine of original sin, and that is because the Bible makes it clear that men are born in a state of fallenness and corruption. But Jonathan Edwards speculated, in his essay on original sin, that even if the Bible never said a word about original sin, it is such a distinct characteristic of human beings that reason itself would have to conclude that it exists, in order to account for the universality of sin. Why is this the case? The philosopher Jean-Jacques Rousseau said that man is born innocent, but by exposure to the world, he comes to be bound, enslaved—he is corrupted by civilization. The corrupting dimension of civilization is other human beings. But, how can a civilization become corrupt unless the individuals within it are corrupt? Edwards said that if man is born neutral with respect to evil and virtue, you would expect that at least 50 percent of the people in the world would never sin. How do we account for the fact that everyone is tarnished? We even violate our own standards of ethics. Edwards said every human being is born with a predisposition to wickedness.

Pelagius went on to say that, not only can man resist sin, he can resist it easily, and—though he recognized that the grace of God facilitates goodness—grace is not necessary to achieve goodness. He understood grace primarily in terms of instruction: all people need in order to be righteous is to be taught the difference between right and wrong. The reality is, though, that it's not enough to teach children the difference between right and wrong, as parents know, because we still have to deal with the commitment in the heart and soul to do what is evil. God creates a being, stamps His own image and likeness onto that being, and gives that person dominion over all of the earth—and then, day after day, that person lives a life of estrangement and disobedience to God.

That's who we are in our natural state. Does that concern you? The gap between the righteousness of God and the unrighteousness of His image bearers is a serious problem. God commands us to be perfect, and we are not perfect. What do we do about it?

Here are some of the options. You can deny that you're imperfect; then you don't have to worry about it. You can deny it by rationalizing your own sin, or by minimizing your sin. Another thing you can do is to minimize God's holiness, to assume that He is not perfect. If He's not perfect, then He won't be bothered by imperfections in you. Or, of course, you can deny the existence of God altogether.

For all practical purposes, it doesn't matter whether you deny God altogether or simply strip Him of some troublesome attributes, the chief of which is His holiness. As long as He's not a holy God, the god you're talking about is not the one true God. But we will do anything in our power to escape the obvious impasse between a righteous Creator and an unrighteous creature. The whole message of the Christian faith is that humankind, in the fullness of our humanity, needs redemption. We need a Savior. We need someone who can deal with the very core of our humanity, who can enter into the human condition and acquire what we desperately need for ourselves—righteousness. That's why Jesus' perfect humanity is absolutely essential for us.

Sometimes people argue about whether Christianity can be the only way to God. What about other world religions? There's one thing that Christianity has that no other religion has: an atonement. The fundamental issue that Christianity addresses is not morality or liturgy; what Christianity addresses is the problem of guilt. It takes guilt seriously, because it takes man seriously, and it provides a Savior who gives us a new humanity, and who begins to clear away the fog on the image that we bear—cleaning it up, erasing the defects, reshaping it to bring us into conformity to Christ, so that in looking at us, people can begin to see a likeness of the character of God. In His mercy, God has made a way to be reconciled to Him and to have the obscured image of God restored in those who trust in Christ alone for salvation—so that we may bring Him glory and show forth His holiness to creation once more.

About the Author

Dr. R.C. Sproul was founder of Ligonier Ministries, founding pastor of Saint Andrew's Chapel in Sanford, Fla., first president of Reformation Bible College, and executive editor of *Tabletalk* magazine. His radio program, *Renewing Your Mind*, is still broadcast daily on hundreds of radio stations around the world and can also be heard online. He was author of more than one hundred books, including *The Holiness of God, Chosen by God,* and *Everyone's a Theologian.* He was recognized throughout the world for his articulate defense of the inerrancy of Scripture and the need for God's people to stand with conviction upon His Word.

Get 3 free months
of *Tabletalk*

In 1977, R.C. Sproul started *Tabletalk* magazine.
Today it has become the most widely read subscriber-based monthly
devotional magazine in the world. **Try it free for 3 months.**

TryTabletalk.com/CQ | 800-435-4343